Adapted and published in the United States
in 1986 by Silver Burdett Company,
Morristown, New Jersey

A TEMPLAR BOOK
Devised and produced by Templar Publishing Ltd,
Old King's Head Court, Dorking, Surrey.

Library of Congress Cataloging-in-Publication Data
Stidworthy, John, 1943–
    Mighty mammals of the past.

    (Creatures from the past)
    Summary: Describes what the fossilized remains of
mammals that lived before, during and after the Age
of Dinosaurs have revealed about their physical
characteristics and way of life.
    1. Mammals, Fossil—Juvenile literature
[1. Mammals, Fossil] I. Parker, Steve. II. Forsey,
Christopher, ill. III. Title. IV. Series.
QE881.S674   1986   569   86-10211
ISBN 0-382-09321-6

Series editor: A J Wood
Editor: Nicholas Bellenberg
Designer: Mike Jolley
Production: Sandra Bennigsen

Origination: Anglia Reproductions, Witham, Essex
Printing: Purnell (Book Production) Ltd, Paulton, Bristol,
        Member of BPCC plc

PICTURE CREDITS
Page 6: Science Photo Library
Page 10: The Mansell Collection
Page 35: Mary Evans Picture Library

MIGHTY MAMMALS OF THE PAST

Written by
JOHN STIDWORTHY
MA (Cambridge)

Consultant Editor
STEVE PARKER
BSc Zoology

Illustrated by
CHRIS FORSEY

SILVER BURDETT COMPANY

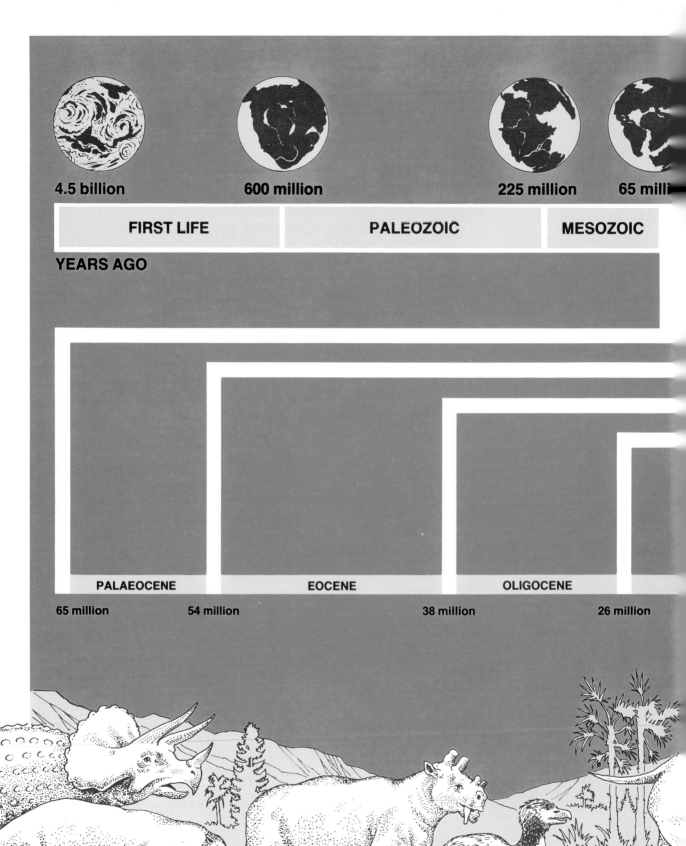

4.5 billion   **600 million**   **225 million**   **65 milli**

| FIRST LIFE | PALEOZOIC | MESOZOIC |

YEARS AGO

PALAEOCENE   EOCENE   OLIGOCENE

65 million   **54 million**   **38 million**   **26 million**

Today

**CENOZOIC
HE AGE OF MAMMALS**

MIOCENE   **PLIOCENE**

7 million   **2 million**

CONTENTS

THE FIRST MAMMALS

Sixty-five million years ago, dinosaurs suddenly became extinct. How suddenly we may never know. It was quick in terms of the fossil record in the rocks, but it happened so long ago that it's almost impossible for us to tell if they died out over a few months or thousands of years.

What is certain is that the dinosaurs, which had been the biggest, most successful and probably the brainiest animals to live on this planet for more than 100 million years, were completely wiped out. Many other living things also died, including over half the plants and lots of the surface-dwelling sea creatures. But some things managed to survive, and the disappearance of the dinosaurs provided them with a great opportunity to take over the Earth. The creatures that took this opportunity were the mammals.

Mammals were already around during and even before the Age of Dinosaurs. But they were mostly small, nocturnal animals that spent their time scampering through the undergrowth or climbing trees in order to hide from the hunting dinosaurs. Mammals seemed to have no way of challenging the dinosaurs for supremacy. But once the dinosaurs disappeared, they got their chance. Mammals quickly took over the land and became the dominant animals. The last 65 million years – and perhaps the next few million – are all part of the Age of Mammals.

Iridium in clay
In the photo above you can see the clay layer containing iridium (marked by a coin) that was formed during the Cretaceous period and discovered by scientists just a few years ago.

Death by meteorite

A layer of clay, containing a lot of the rare metal iridium, has been discovered in various parts of the Earth's crust. This has led scientists to believe that a huge meteorite – estimated to be 6 miles across – may once have crashed into our planet, as iridium is rare on Earth but common in meteorites. The dust and rocks thrown into the air when it crashed, would have stopped heat and light from the Sun reaching the Earth, and may have led to the death of the dinosaurs.

What could have happened 65 million years ago to kill the dinosaurs? There are many suggestions, but some of them are difficult to believe. One theory says the dinosaurs were too stupid to survive, but modern evidence shows they were the most advanced creatures of their time. Some had large brains and were probably quite smart. Another explanation is that disease wiped them out – but it's hard to imagine a disease that could affect so many different kinds of animal all at once.

One big problem is that the theory must explain not only the death of the dinosaurs, but also the disappearance of many other kinds of animals and plants. At the same time the dinosaurs were dying, so were most of the large non-dinosaur reptiles that lived on the land. Pterodactyls, some kinds of plants, and sea creatures also vanished.

The most likely explanation for all this death and destruction is that there were great changes in climate. It is possible that a massive meteorite crashed into the Earth, throwing up huge clouds of dust that blotted out the Sun. Another theory is that the dinosaurs died out over a much longer period, as a result of normal changes to the climate and also

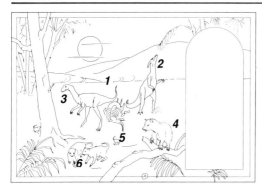

North America at the end of the Age of Dinosaurs

1 Triceratops *was a plant-eating dinosaur that grazed in herds.*

2 Thescelosaurus *was another plant-eating dinosaur – a new type that appeared near the end of the Age of Dinosaurs.*

3 Stenonychosaurus *was a meat-eating dinosaur about the size of a human being. It may have hunted small mammals at night.*

4 Didelphodon *was a marsupial similar to today's opossums.*

5 *Insect-eating mammals resembling today's shrews lived alongside the dinosaurs for millions of years.*

6 *Many small plant-eating mammals belonged to the group called multituberculates, but became extinct as more modern mammals appeared.*

changes in the sea level. Some scientists have looked for a connection with the amount of heat and light coming from the Sun which could have made the dinosaurs too cold or too hot. A few have suggested that our Sun has a twin, which usually remains hidden behind the normal Sun, but comes out every now and then to overheat the Earth.

You may have guessed by now that the real truth is that we do not know what caused the death of the dinosaurs and the other animals and plants! We may never find out for sure, but digging up clues and piecing together evidence is certainly exciting work.

A cooling climate

65 million-year old fossils found in Montana show the Earth's climate changed a lot over half a million years.

The fossils show us that warm subtropical forests, like the one below, which were home for lots of dinosaurs, became replaced with cool pine forests and a completely different mixture of animals. This may have happened due to changes in the climate caused by the continents drifting and altering sea levels.

How to say...

Triceratops
Try-serra-tops

Thescelosaurus
Thes-kell-oh-sore-us

Stenonychosaurus
Sten-on-iko-sore-us

Didelphodon
Die-dell-fow-don

Too hot for comfort

Some fossil dinosaur eggs from late in the Age of Dinosaurs have been found to have extremely thin shells.

Today, birds lay thin shelled eggs if they are diseased, poisoned, or if the climate around them is too hot. Was this the case for the dinosaurs? Perhaps the Earth became very hot – due to the appearance of another Sun, or our Sun becoming very active.

If this happened, the increase in temperature would have killed the dinosaurs, since they were unable to cool themselves, and it would also have affected the sea-dwelling creatures.

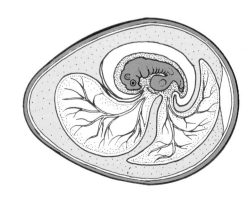

Did they all die?
If cold killed the dinosaurs, perhaps a few survived where the climate stayed warm – in parts of tropical Africa, for example. Most scientists cannot believe that there are still a few dinosaurs alive on the Earth, but even today there are stories of unknown beasts living in remote swamps, and huge creatures hiding away in the depths of dark lagoons. Could it be that they are the last survivors of the Age of Dinosaurs?

The first mammals

We may not know why the dinosaurs died out. But do we know why mammals took over? Before we can answer that question, we must decide what a mammal is. The main features to look out for are shown on the right. Most important is the fact that mammals are warm-blooded. They keep their bodies at a constant temperature, and are ready for action at all times, and in all weather. The reptiles (including the dinosaurs) were cold-blooded and needed to soak up heat energy from the sun before they could move about. Lots of them were very big so they absorbed heat slowly, but once they became warm they had no way of cooling themselves down if the climate became too hot. This could

be why the mammals survived 65 million years ago while the dinosaurs perished through overheating or by being frozen to death.

Although fossils can't tell us if a prehistoric animal was warm-blooded, they do give us a few clues. By looking at an animal's bones – the main parts usually preserved as fossils – we can often figure out whether or not it was a mammal.

You can see from the chart below that scientists have found a whole series of fossil animals which gradually change from reptiles to mammals. We must draw a line somewhere and say: "All animals with these features are mammals." Most fossil experts agree that if an animal is found to have a single bone for its lower jaw and three small bones in each ear, then we can call it a mammal.

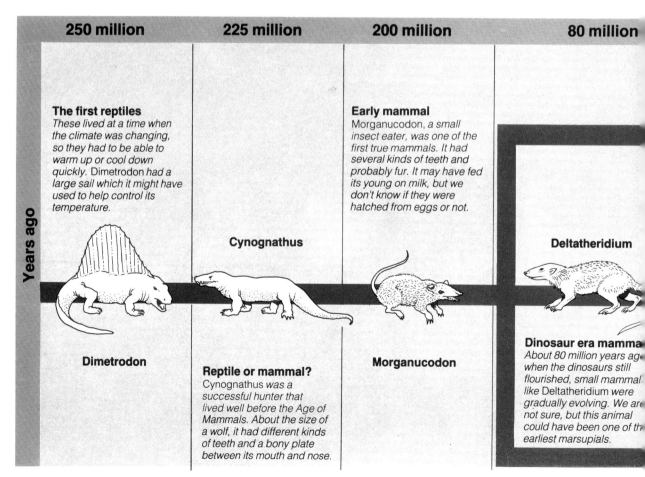

250 million | **225 million** | **200 million** | **80 million**

Years ago

The first reptiles
These lived at a time when the climate was changing, so they had to be able to warm up or cool down quickly. Dimetrodon had a large sail which it might have used to help control its temperature.

Dimetrodon

Cynognathus

Reptile or mammal?
Cynognathus was a successful hunter that lived well before the Age of Mammals. About the size of a wolf, it had different kinds of teeth and a bony plate between its mouth and nose.

Early mammal
Morganucodon, a small insect eater, was one of the first true mammals. It had several kinds of teeth and probably fur. It may have fed its young on milk, but we don't know if they were hatched from eggs or not.

Morganucodon

Deltatheridium

Dinosaur era mamma
About 80 million years ag when the dinosaurs still flourished, small mammal like Deltatheridium were gradually evolving. We are not sure, but this animal could have been one of th earliest marsupials.

What is a mammal?

Here is a typical mammal. It has fur, keeps warm and stays active, but to do this it needs lots of fuel (food) and a continuous supply of oxygen (from the air). The bony plate which separates the nose from the mouth means it can breathe and chew at the same time, for oxygen and food. Also it gives birth to babies, instead of laying eggs like a reptile. The babies are cared for and fed with milk by the mother. These and many other improvements over the reptiles meant that mammals could take over the world 65 million years ago.

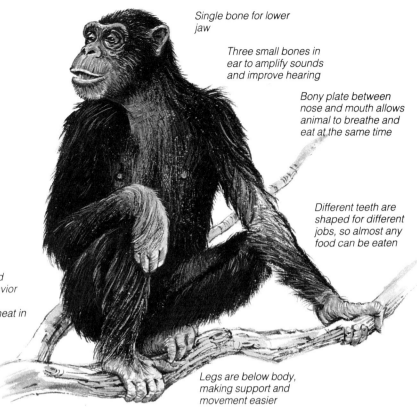

Single bone for lower jaw

Three small bones in ear to amplify sounds and improve hearing

Bony plate between nose and mouth allows animal to breathe and eat at the same time

Different teeth are shaped for different jobs, so almost any food can be eaten

Large brain and intelligent behavior

Fur keeps body heat in

In a placental mammal, the young are born quite well-formed and are fed on milk from the mother's nipples

Legs are below body, making support and movement easier

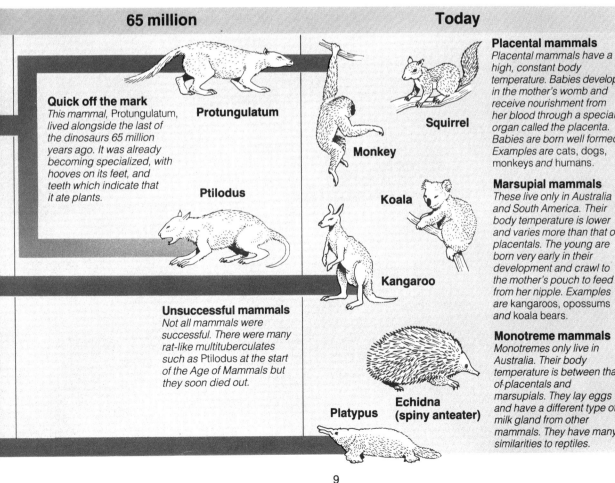

65 million   Today

Quick off the mark
This mammal, Protungulatum, lived alongside the last of the dinosaurs 65 million years ago. It was already becoming specialized, with hooves on its feet, and teeth which indicate that it ate plants.

Protungulatum

Ptilodus

Unsuccessful mammals
Not all mammals were successful. There were many rat-like multituberculates such as Ptilodus at the start of the Age of Mammals but they soon died out.

Squirrel

Monkey

Koala

Kangaroo

Platypus   **Echidna (spiny anteater)**

Placental mammals
Placental mammals have a high, constant body temperature. Babies develop in the mother's womb and receive nourishment from her blood through a special organ called the placenta. Babies are born well formed. Examples are cats, dogs, monkeys and humans.

Marsupial mammals
These live only in Australia and South America. Their body temperature is lower and varies more than that of placentals. The young are born very early in their development and crawl to the mother's pouch to feed from her nipple. Examples are kangaroos, opossums and koala bears.

Monotreme mammals
Monotremes only live in Australia. Their body temperature is between that of placentals and marsupials. They lay eggs and have a different type of milk gland from other mammals. They have many similarities to reptiles.

Who was Cuvier?

Frenchman Georges Cuvier (1769 – 1832) was the first real palaeontologist (fossil expert). He had an amazing knowledge of living creatures, on which he based his fossil work. He was able to tell which fossil mammals were related to living ones, and deduce appearances from a single bone.

How do fossils form?

Most dead animals and plants are eaten or rot away, leaving no trace of their existence. Just occasionally, however, an animal dies and its body somehow ends up in a river or swamp, where it is soon covered by mud and buried. Even then the body may decay but, if conditions are right, the hard parts like bones and teeth will be preserved. For thousands or millions of years they stay there – until one day they are discovered by a lucky fossil-hunter. Fossils, then, are the remains of long-dead animals and plants.

Hard parts such as bones and teeth may be unchanged when they are dug up, thousands of years after the animal has died. But usually chemical changes will have taken place, even though the size and shape of the original will have been preserved. Minerals seep in and harden the bone tissues, or water dissolves away the original material, replacing it with new minerals. Sometimes the bone is completely dissolved away, leaving only a hole in the rock. Later, this hole may be filled by a different material seeping into it, filling the place of the original remains. Rarely, is a whole animal preserved, trapped in amber or pickled in natural tar.

As well as the remains of actual animals, scientists have also discovered another type of fossil, called a trace fossil. This is a preserved trace or sign of an animal rather than the creature itself. Footprints, the marks where it rested or fed, or even fossil droppings are all trace fossils.

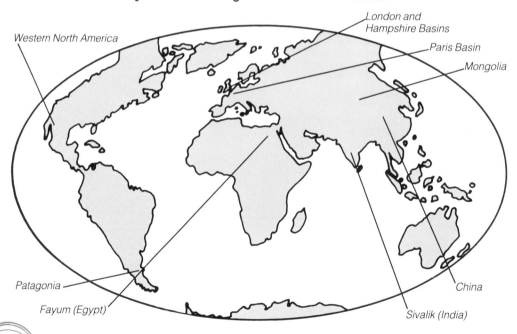

Western North America
London and Hampshire Basins
Paris Basin
Mongolia
Patagonia
Fayum (Egypt)
China
Sivalik (India)

Where to look for fossils

Fossils are usually found in sedimentary rocks formed from the mud in lakes, rivers, and seas. Look for fossil-bearing rocks in cliffs, riverbanks, and excavations, but be careful as these places can be dangerous. Remember, too, that you may need permission to visit quarries and excavations.

The fossils described in this book nearly all come from fairly "new" rocks – formed in the last 65 million years. If you go looking for fossils, you are most likely to find those of sea creatures such as shellfish, since mammal fossils are rare. Those embedded in rocks will have to be removed with a geological hammer. Try and split the rocks along natural breaks, or else you'll probably just destroy them.

The making of fossils

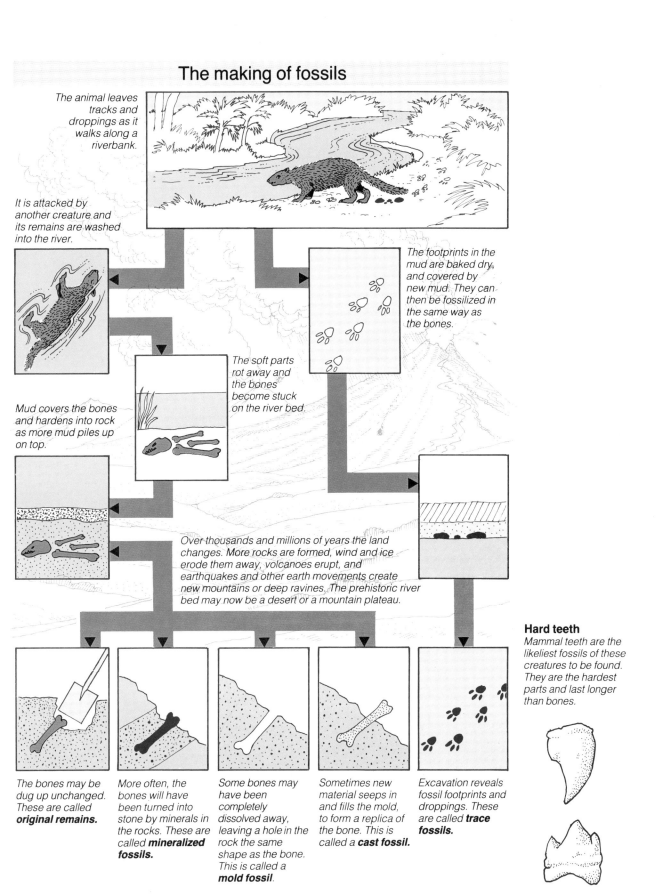

The animal leaves tracks and droppings as it walks along a riverbank.

It is attacked by another creature and its remains are washed into the river.

The footprints in the mud are baked dry, and covered by new mud. They can then be fossilized in the same way as the bones.

The soft parts rot away and the bones become stuck on the river bed.

Mud covers the bones and hardens into rock as more mud piles up on top.

Over thousands and millions of years the land changes. More rocks are formed, wind and ice erode them away, volcanoes erupt, and earthquakes and other earth movements create new mountains or deep ravines. The prehistoric river bed may now be a desert or a mountain plateau.

The bones may be dug up unchanged. These are called **original remains.**

More often, the bones will have been turned into stone by minerals in the rocks. These are called **mineralized fossils.**

Some bones may have been completely dissolved away, leaving a hole in the rock the same shape as the bone. This is called a **mold fossil**.

Sometimes new material seeps in and fills the mold, to form a replica of the bone. This is called a **cast fossil.**

Excavation reveals fossil footprints and droppings. These are called **trace fossils.**

Hard teeth
Mammal teeth are the likeliest fossils of these creatures to be found. They are the hardest parts and last longer than bones.

11

ALL SHAPES AND SIZES

Fifty million years ago, during the early Eocene period, the dinosaurs had all disappeared. But their place was quickly filled by mammals of all shapes and sizes. Birds, too, evolved rapidly. Giant flightless birds like *Diatryma* stalked the Earth, probably attacking and eating small mammals. But the birds soon lost the battle for supremacy on the ground, and mammals became the main land animals.

Although many mammals from 50 million years ago were quite different from those alive now, their surroundings were becoming increasingly like our own. The flowers and trees were similar to the varieties alive now, and much of the Earth was forest. There were no wide, grassy plains, though, since grasses had not yet appeared.

Eocene fossils have given us clues that tell us that many parts of the world were much warmer than they are today. Warmth-loving fig trees and magnolias grew in Alaska. Crocodiles and turtles swam among palm trees in the swamps of southern England. And in most of Britain the climate was like Malaysia's is now.

Compared to modern mammals, many Eocene mammals look odd and clumsy. But we must remember that evolution works slowly, and that these animals were fairly new to their way of life. We can think of them as "experimental" mammals which evolution was trying out in a world suddenly free of dinosaurs.

Protungulatum

Ectoconus

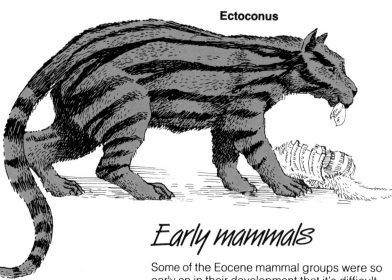

Weird and wonderful mammals

From 54 to 38 million years ago, during the Eocene period, the mammals developed rapidly. Those that had shared the Earth with the dinosaurs continued to survive and were joined by many new species. Before long a new set of weird and wonderful beasts had evolved to take advantage of the food and living spaces once used by the dinosaurs.

We have found out all this from the evidence of fossils. Many of the best Eocene fossils come from North America. Some more have been discovered in South America and Africa. The fossils tell us that some of the new mammal designs were very successful and existed for many millions of years. But other creatures came and went in a much shorter time. Some fossils show the remains of animals which have no equivalents today, making it difficult for us to imagine what they were like.

Quite early on in the Age of Mammals, all the main groups of mammals had appeared. These groups are called *orders*. During the Eocene there were 25 orders, perhaps more. Today there are about 17 orders. So you can see that some of those early mammal "designs" obviously didn't survive, while others gradually evolved into the mammals that live in the world today.

Early mammals

Some of the Eocene mammal groups were so early on in their development that it's difficult for palaeontologists to tell them apart. Many groups evolved from the same ancestors and looked very similar, even though their modern descendants are quite different. Early hoofed mammals like *Protungulatum* (top), which ate plants, looked very much like their hunting, meat-eating cousin *Ectoconus* (above). In the millions of years since then, these two groups have become more and more different, so that today they are represented by deer and tigers — much easier to tell apart!

North America in the early Eocene

1 Phenacodus *had tiny hoofs on its toes. Its short legs and weak teeth indicate that it probably ate only the softest leaves and shoots.*

2 Oxyaena *was an early kind of meat-eater called a* creodont. *It had sharp slicing teeth, flat feet and a small brain.*

3 Uintatherium *was the biggest mammal of its time, but has no present-day relatives. It browsed on tree leaves.*

4 Notharctus *was a very early kind of lemur, and may be an ancestor of modern lemurs.*

5 Diatryma *was a giant flightless bird. It could have used its sharp, strong beak for tearing apart other creatures, but some experts think that* Diatryma *was a vegetarian.*

14

Flippers and wings

During the Eocene, mammals became very specialized, some taking to the water, others to the air. The primitive whale *Basilosaurus* swam in the oceans, its legs having evolved into flippers. The first bats took to the skies, having developed wings of skin held out by the bones of their hands. And, like the bats of today, they had become specially adapted to hang upside-down when resting. In fact, bats have changed very little over the millions of years since they first appeared. Their design is much the same today as it was then.

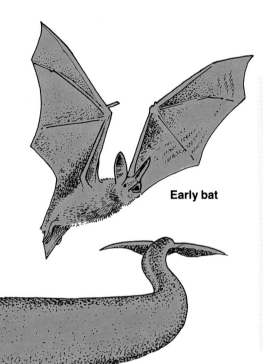

Early bat

Basilosaurus

How to say...

Phenacodus
Fen-a-code-us

Oxyaena
Ox-eye-eena

Uintatherium
Winta-theer-ee-um

Notharctus
No-thark-tus

Diatryma
Die-a-try-ma

Andrewsarchus
Andrew-sark-us

Coryphodon
Korry-foe-don

Giants of the Eocene

Some Eocene mammals took over from the dinosaurs as the giants of the animal world. The rhino-like *Uintatherium* on page 12 was 6 feet tall and nearly 14 feet long – about the size of a pick-up truck!

In this panel you can see two more giants of the Eocene. *Andrewsarchus* has no living relatives, so the only clues we have to its way of life come from fossils. We can tell that it had rounded teeth and a heavy body – like a modern bear. So some experts think that it ate the same sort of food – almost anything! Others say it ate dead animals, thinking that it was similar to a hyena. *Coryphodon* was one of the largest herbivores.

Coryphodon, from Europe and North America, was a plant-eater 8¼ feet long.

This fearsome beast is called Andrewsarchus, *and it lived in what is now Mongolia. Its skull alone was 3 feet long.*

Mammal meat eaters

As more and more mammals came along they took to new ways of life. Some groups evolved to become plant-eaters, or *herbivores*, grazing in herds or browsing on the leaves of trees. It wasn't long before other mammals worked out that the herbivores themselves were a new source of food. So the meat-eaters, or *carnivores*, evolved.

Over millions of years the carnivores generally became bigger, so that they could tackle larger prey. They also developed large, sharp teeth so they could catch hold of and cut up their victims. Many carnivores that were a success during most of the Eocene belonged to one particular group – the *creodonts*.

The word creodont means "flesh tooth." The creodonts evolved from the small, insect-eating mammals like *Deltatheridium*, which were alive at the time of the last dinosaurs. During the Eocene, creodonts gradually became larger, and their teeth became bigger and sharper for dealing with meat. They developed big slicing, *carnassial*, teeth at the back of their mouths to act as shears for cutting tough skin and flesh.

Most creodonts had long, low heads with room for only a small, primitive brain. So they were probably not very smart. Many also had the old-fashioned type of mammal feet, where the sole and five toes were placed flat on the ground. A few stood up on their toes – a more advanced design for fast running.

As evolution continued the old-fashioned, slow and clumsy herbivores gradually disappeared or changed into quicker, cleverer versions. It is thought that the creodonts, which had a fairly primitive design and small brains, could not keep up with the changes. They gradually died out, and by 38 million years ago were nearly all extinct. Scientific evidence shows that modern meat eaters actually evolved from a different mammal group called *fissipeds*.

Fight for food
Here a creodont *lives up to its "flesh tooth" name. A* Tritemnodon *sets about making a meal of a* Notharctus.

16

Patriofelis

Oxyaenids

The oxyaenids were one of the two main groups of creodonts. They had short, squat skulls, short legs and flat feet which probably ended in blunt, rounded claws. *Oxyaena*, which gave its name to the group, was about the size of a badger but slimmer (see page 12). It could have killed animals up to the size of a rabbit, and possibly tried to catch larger prey. *Patriofelis*, shown here, was a medium-sized, cat-like creodont. *Megistotherium* was a giant creodont as big as a rhino. It was one of the few members of the creodont group to survive until the Miocene, 20 million years ago, and can be seen on page 27.

Hyaenodontids

This group of creodonts had long skulls and jaws and tended to stand on their toes. They were generally fairly small. *Hyaenodon* was one member of the group, and is shown on page 18. *Tritemnodon* (on the right) was another – a very slim, muscular animal that could probably outrun most other creatures of its time.

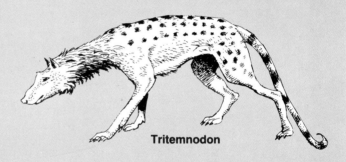
Tritemnodon

What is it?

Mesonyx was another primitive meat eater. It was once thought to be the ancestor of modern carnivorous mammals, which are in the group called *Carnivora*. Then scientists changed their minds and put this creature into the creodont group. More recently opinions have changed again. Scientists now believe that *Mesonyx* was in fact a member of the condylarths, like *Andrewsarchus* on page 15. In another 20 years maybe things will have changed yet again...

Mesonyx

Truly a carnivore

Pseudocynodictis was one of the early fissipeds – the true carnivores that are the ancestors of today's cats, dogs, otters, weasels and many other meat eaters. This slim, swift creature lived around 35 million years ago. It was the size of a large fox and probably led a fox-like way of life, hunting rabbits, rats, mice, and other small creatures.

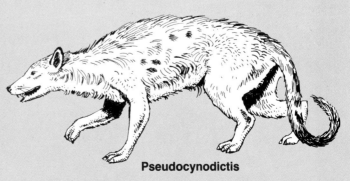
Pseudocynodictis

A TIME OF CHANGE

The Oligocene period, from 38 to 26 million years ago was a time of many changes. After the initial "burst" of evolution early in the Age of Mammals, the groups were sorting themselves out. There were several surprisingly modern-looking types among the animals. The cats for example – the most specialized of the meat eaters – had developed rapidly, and were already very similar to the cats of today. They and other advancing groups were replacing the "old fashioned" mammals such as the creodonts.

Confusingly, some mammals looked like those alive now, but were not close relatives. *Archaeotherium* was like a large pig but it belonged to the entelodonts, a separate group from the one which gave rise to present-day pigs, giraffes, antelopes, and other mammals with an even number of toes on each foot.

Other Oligocene animals were the ancestors of species around today, but they had not yet evolved into the typical shapes we would recognize. *Poebrotherium*, no bigger than a sheep, was a small, early type of camel that already had just two toes on each foot – like today's camels.

Some Oligocene creatures – like *Merycoidodon*, which looked like a cross between a pig and a sheep – were very successful at the time, but died out. The Oligocene was an interesting phase in mammal evolution, and it presents palaeontologists with plenty of puzzles.

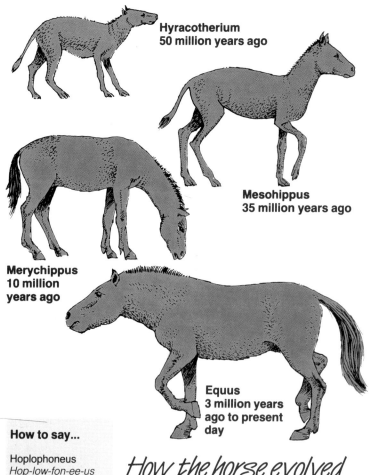

Hyracotherium
50 million years ago

Mesohippus
35 million years ago

Merychippus
10 million years ago

Equus
3 million years ago to present day

The great Oligocene success story involved the group of mammals which are called "perissodactyl ungulates" – hoofed mammals with an odd number of toes on each foot. These are the horses, rhinos, and tapirs. During the Oligocene they flourished in a way that has never been seen before or since.

When we gather together all the fossils of a certain group, such as horses or rhinos, it is tempting to arrange them in an "evolutionary tree". We may expect the tree to be nice and neat, with just a few tidy branches. We imagine one species evolving into another, which is the ancestor of the next, and so on, in a line up to the present day.

Unfortunately, nature is rarely so straightforward. The simple "tree" is in reality a complicated, twiggy bush. The fossils we find are only the tips of a few twigs; the rest is guesswork based on the evidence discovered. And even though we can place animals in an "evolutionary line," like the rhinos shown opposite, this does not mean that each creature in the line is the ancestor of the one after it. Sometimes they may be. In other cases they probably aren't. We can never know for sure. If someone digs up a completely new kind of fossil the experts may have to draw up the evolutionary trees all over again.

How to say...

Hoplophoneus
Hop-low-fon-ee-us

Archaeotherium
Ark-ee-owe-theer-ee-um

Poebrotherium
Poe-ee-bro-theer-ee-um

Merycoidodon
Merry-coy-doe-don

Hyaenodon
High-een-owe-don

How the horse evolved

50 million years ago, the first horse-like creatures lived in Eocene forests. They were only just bigger than a domestic cat, with five tiny nails on each foot.

Fossils through the ages show that members of the horse group gradually became bigger, with longer and thinner legs. The number of toes on each foot was five, then three, and today it's one – the horse's hoof. The teeth and jaws became bigger and better at dealing with tough foods such as grass. Today the wild horse is a fast-moving, plains-dwelling, herd-living creature.

Nightfall at an American river during the Oligocene

1 Hoplophoneus *was an early saber-toothed cat. Its long canine teeth were used to stab and kill its prey.*

2 Archaeotherium *had tusk-like canine teeth. Fossilized examples suggest that it may have used them to dig and grub up roots.*

3 Poebrotherium *was a very early kind of camel. It was only 20 inches tall at the shoulder.*

4 Merycoidodon *has no descendants living today. Its teeth show it to be related to cud-chewers like cows.*

5 Hyaenodon *was a meat-eating creodont. It was large and heavily built, like today's wolves.*

6 *Prehistoric bats flitted over the dark river, searching for flies and other insects. Bats had already been around for millions of years.*

Rhinos through the ages

Rhinos developed from an early tapir-like animal and the prehistoric ones came in all shapes and sizes. Some didn't have horns, others had one or more. Of the dozens which have lived in the past, there are only five species left alive today. They are all rare, partly because they are hunted by humans. It would be terrible if we were responsible for making them extinct, thus finishing the "rhino tree" forever.

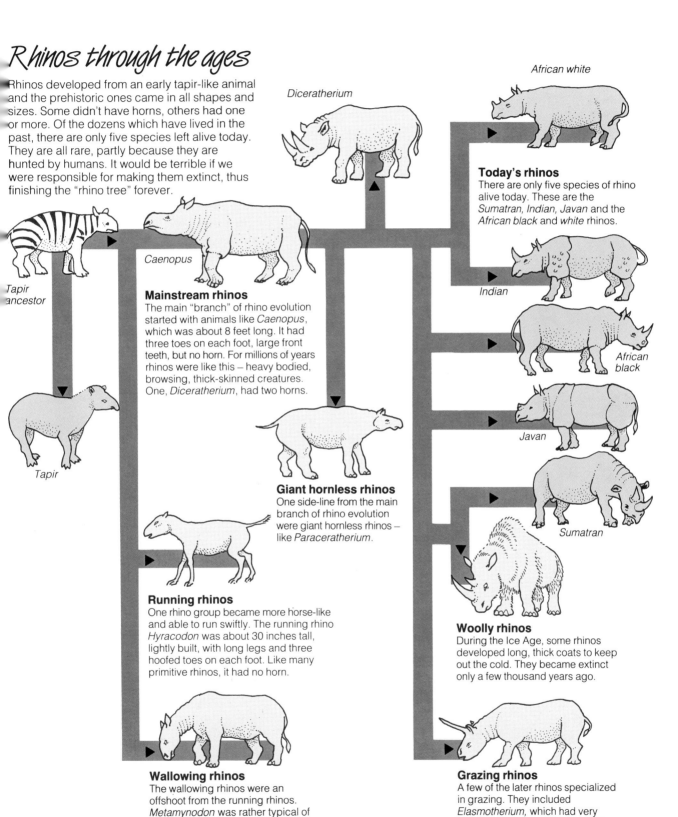

Diceratherium

African white

Caenopus

Tapir ancestor

Today's rhinos
There are only five species of rhino alive today. These are the *Sumatran, Indian, Javan* and the *African black* and *white* rhinos.

Indian

African black

Javan

Sumatran

Mainstream rhinos
The main "branch" of rhino evolution started with animals like *Caenopus*, which was about 8 feet long. It had three toes on each foot, large front teeth, but no horn. For millions of years rhinos were like this – heavy bodied, browsing, thick-skinned creatures. One, *Diceratherium*, had two horns.

Tapir

Giant hornless rhinos
One side-line from the main branch of rhino evolution were giant hornless rhinos – like *Paraceratherium*.

Running rhinos
One rhino group became more horse-like and able to run swiftly. The running rhino *Hyracodon* was about 30 inches tall, lightly built, with long legs and three hoofed toes on each foot. Like many primitive rhinos, it had no horn.

Woolly rhinos
During the Ice Age, some rhinos developed long, thick coats to keep out the cold. They became extinct only a few thousand years ago.

Wallowing rhinos
The wallowing rhinos were an offshoot from the running rhinos. *Metamynodon* was rather typical of this group – rather tubby and short-legged. We think that they swam and wallowed in water, much like hippos do today.

Grazing rhinos
A few of the later rhinos specialized in grazing. They included *Elasmotherium,* which had very strong grinding teeth. This was the largest of the horned rhinos, with a huge horn 6 feet long on a strong skull 3 feet long.

A giant among giants

The biggest mammal that ever lived on land was a giant hornless rhino from 30 million years ago. Its name was *Paraceratherium* and you can see it in the picture below. These giants evolved in Asia during the Oligocene and survived for millions of years. Opposite, you can see two more giants that lived at the same time.

Paraceratherium was a vast animal, over twice the size of today's elephants. It stood 18 feet high at the shoulder, was over 26 feet long, and must have weighed around 18 tons. It had a long neck but a small head for its size. Even so, when it stretched up, the end of its snout could have been 23 feet or more above the ground – easily high enough to reach up to the roof of an ordinary house.

This giant's skull was 4¼ feet long, rather low, with a curious dome in the middle. The front teeth were small tusk-like cones. Behind them in the jaw was a gap, then came the cheek teeth (premolars and molars) which were flat and adapted to crushing leaves. The lack of bone at the front of the skull suggests that the upper lip was long and grasping, maybe like that of today's African black rhino.

Paraceratherium needed strong pillar-like legs to support its weight, but these were by no means fat and clumsy. In fact, this giant was probably quite nimble despite its huge size.

Sprightly giants
Although large, Paraceratherium *was probably very agile. Here a herd of these creatures browse on bushes and trees, grasping the leaves with their pointed lips.*

Double horned giants

On the right you can see two more giants from the Oligocene. *Arsinoitherium* lived in Africa. It was a clumsy plant eater over 11 feet long and had huge double horns on its head. It is likely that it used its horns for self-defense and perhaps in battles over territories and mates.

Brontotherium was one of the biggest titanotheres, measuring over 8 feet at the shoulder. These creatures were descended from the same group as horses. As the "titan" part of their name suggests, many were very large, and were common in many parts of the world some 35 million years ago. No one has been able to decide why *Brontotherium* had such a large bony double horn, but one theory is that it developed as a result of *allometry*. This is when one part of a creature's body develops at a different rate from the rest.

For instance, over a few million years an animal's body might become twice the size of its ancestors – but its horn could grow to four times as big. This process of allometry has happened in many different animal groups, but we are not sure how it occurs. The illustrations below show how we imagine it may have happened in *Brontotherium*.

Arsinoitherium

Brontotherium

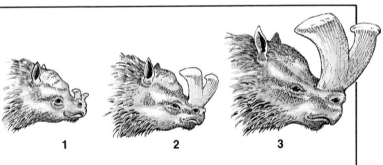

1   2   3

1 *Ancestor of* Brontotherium, *with small body and horn.*

2 Brontotherium, *with large body and very large horn.*

3 *Suppose* Brontotherium *had lived on and evolved for a few more million years. Its horns would have continued to grow at a much faster rate than its body...then they would have been absolutely gigantic!*

LIFE ON THE PLAINS

The animals that live in our modern world are greatly affected by the plants growing in their environment. This was also true during prehistoric times. During the long period called the Miocene, which was from 26 to 7 million years ago, grasses became important plants. This was because the climate in many parts of the world became drier, so the drought-resistant grasslands spread as the rain-loving forests died back.

As the plants changed, so did the animals. Shady forest glades with their succulent leaves, shoots, and fruits gave way to open plains of tough grass, and animals needed tough teeth to make use of it. It was a case of "browsers out, grazers in." Many of the old-style browsing mammals became less common and new types, grazing on the grasses and other ground-growing plants, took over.

At the start of the Miocene there were still many types of rhino, but the other main group of odd-toed hoofed mammals, the horses, became much more widespread. The even-toed hoofed mammals also became numerous, many of them living in herds.

By the end of the period plains-dwelling herbivores such as antelopes were in existence, along with deer and giraffes. A new selection of carnivores evolved to prey on these new plant eaters. The world was changing, and the mammals, ever adaptable, were changing with it.

How to say...

Syndyoceras
Sin-dee-owe-sare-us

Alticamelus
Alt-ee-camel-us

Diceratherium
Die-sare-a-theer-ee-um

Daphoenodon
Daff-een-owe-don

Moropus
Morrow-puss

Lifestyles of long ago

The idea that certain parts of a living thing develop to carry out a particular task is a cornerstone of evolutionary thinking. In other words, the job shapes the part. We can see this as we look at today's animals and the food they eat: the long neck of the giraffe, the trunk of the elephant, the claws of the cat, and so on.

This way of thinking can be used with fossils. For example, we can guess at the type of food eaten by a prehistoric mammal by looking at its fossil teeth and skull. Does it have the flat, grinding teeth of a plant eater or the sharp, pointed ones of a carnivore? We can also be more confident about our deductions by making comparisons with present-day animals.

The general size and shape of a fossil mammal can tell us much about its lifestyle. For instance, a bulky creature that weighed several tons, like the

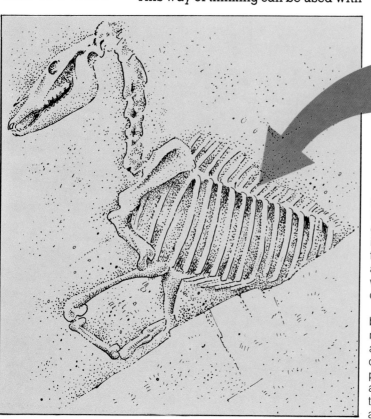

Plant remains

Herds, families and food

Present-day hoofed mammals often live in herds. Finding fossils of ancient mammals in groups leads us to suspect that they also lived in herds, and that they all died together in a flood or similar disaster. If the bones are of just a few adults and youngsters, then the group was probably a family party, rather than a herd of adults with only a few young.

Further aspects of an animal's lifestyle may be guessed from other remains found with or near its fossils. Plant remains, like those shown above, are sometimes found – leaves, seeds or wood from forest trees, or grasses from plains and prairies. If an animal's fossils are always associated with remains of a certain type of plant, then we can guess that the animal probably lived in that sort of habitat.

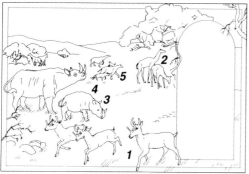

North American prairie during the Miocene

1 Syndyoceras *was an even-toed hoofed mammal. Although rather like an antelope in appearance it belonged to a more primitive group.*

2 Alticamelus *was an early type of camel – probably without a hump. It was about 11 feet tall.*

3 Diceratherium *was a two-horned rhino, one of the "mainstream" rhinos described on page 21.*

4 Daphoenodon *was an early dog of the group sometimes called bear-dogs. It was a little less than 5 feet long with a heavy build and short legs. It probably ate some plant food as well as meat.*

5 Moropus *was an odd mammal related to horses and rhinos, but it had claws on its front feet. As you can read on page 28, we are not at all sure about its way of life.*

Diceratherium on the previous spread, could never have climbed trees. Nor could a long, thin-legged hoofed mammal like *Syndyoceras*. Instead, we can tell from its skeleton that *Syndyoceras* was a runner. This "running leg" design can be seen over and over again, from the fleet-footed dinosaurs to the horses of today. The legs are long, slim, and easy to swing. The strong, leg-moving muscles are concentrated at the top, near the body, while the lower part of the leg is very light, with a long foot and as few toes as possible. This design increases stiffness for a good push-off against the ground, and decreases the number of bones and joints – and so the weight – at the leg's tip. The lighter the lower leg and foot are, the easier and faster they can be swung when running.

We often find fossils of one creature with, or near another. If this happens many times, it's unlikely to be coincidence. Then we can make intelligent guesses about why the fossils are together. For example, fossils of the giant North African creodont *Megistotherium* are often found with the fossilized bones of primitive elephants called mastodons. So we can deduce from this that mastodons were a favorite prey of the huge *Megistotherium*.

Well-suited killer
Megistotherium had huge canine teeth and large attachments for strong muscles to close its jaws. It weighed over 1900 lbs, which makes it the largest flesh-eating mammal known! Here it is attacking a mastodon.

Mammal puzzles

Some mammals from the past are very similar to the mammals of today. Using today's species as examples, we can make good guesses about the prehistoric mammals' way of life. But there are some fossils with no living equivalents, and no close relatives. Several fossils have such an odd appearance or such an unusual combination of features that it is very difficult to guess how they lived, and the scientists argue about them. They may have different ideas about what the animal looked like and how it lived. This is why you may find quite varied pictures of the same animal in different books.

Moropus ("awkward feet") belonged to the group known as chalicotheres, and is one of the most puzzling cases.

Moropus lived during the Miocene and was a distant relative of horses and rhinos. Yet it looks like a "misfit" mammal, made up of spare parts. It had a horse-like head and teeth; its body was massive and heavy; its front legs were longer than its back legs; and its feet had claws rather than hoofs, the front claws being especially large.

Moropus has been reconstructed in several different ways , as you can see here and on page 24. Some experts now believe that it may have shambled along on its front knuckles, rather like a chimpanzee. Its teeth show it to be a herbivore, which leads us to ask what it used its claws for. Did it dig up roots, pull leafy branches to its mouth, or defend itself with them? It's certainly hard for us to tell with such a confusing creature that looks like a cross between a horse, a bear, and an ape.

"Spare parts" mammal

The "spare parts" mammal, *Moropus*, has been constructed from fossils in many ways – as you can read on the opposite page. Here we see it in what scientists now believe is the most likely form.

Stabbers or slashers?

Saber-toothed cats have had a long and varied history, but we can only imagine what they used their long, curving teeth for. These weapons were so long that they could not have snapped shut on prey, in the way that those of modern cats do, and were too delicate to risk stabbing prey with. Instead they may have been used to cut and slash at the victims' neck, so that the main blood vessels were severed. Some people have even suggested that saber-toothed cats fed only on the blood of their prey, pointing out that the very small teeth in the rest of the cat's jaw would have been useless for crunching up gristle or bone.

Macrauchenia is another fossil mammal that has caused many arguments. It used to live in South America and its skeleton shows that it had nostril holes high up on its skull. But scientists have developed three different ideas about *why* they were there.

Some say *Macrauchenia* lived in swamps and that it could submerge itself to escape from danger, leaving just its nostrils above the surface of the water so it could breathe.

Then again, *Macrauchenia* could have had a small trunk for gathering food. But its skull is neater around the nostril holes than those of modern trunked mammals, like elephants and tapirs.

The last and most likely suggestion is that its nostrils could have been closed by muscular flaps to keep out dust and sand – like those of modern camels. If this is true, then this clue leads us to deduce that *Macrauchenia* lived on the sandy plains.

Macrauchenia
Three "incarnations" of the mammal
Macrauchenia:
1 The swamp creature.
2 The elephant look-alike.
3 The plains dweller.

1

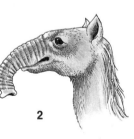

2

3

MAMMALS OF YESTERYEAR

In the Pliocene period, from 7 to 2 million years ago, the mammals of the world were mostly similar to today's. Deer, pigs, giraffes, and many antelope species roamed over Europe, Asia, and probably Africa. They were almost identical to today's versions. In fact in Europe, Asia, and North America, more than three-quarters of the mammals belonged to groups still in existence now, although some of the individual species were different.

Yet in some parts of the world, such as South America and Australia, strange, old-fashioned mammals still survived. And we don't have to look far for the reason. These two continents had been isolated from the rest of the world by stretches of ocean for millions of years. Their mammals had evolved in isolation, developing their own particular mixtures of species.

There were still many primitive *marsupial* (pouched) mammals on these two "island" continents, even though they had long since died out in other parts of the world. Some marsupials, such as the saber-toothed cat *Thylacosmilus*, had developed astonishing similarities to more advanced mammals elsewhere, because they had similar ways of life. Others were quite unique. Today there are still many marsupial species in Australia, and some in South America, but they are under great threat from the more advanced *placental* mammals – including the most "advanced" of all, the human.

Trunks and tusks

For most of the last 35 million years there have been mammals that could be loosely described as "elephants." The steps in elephant evolution are quite complex, so it is difficult to draw up their family tree. What is clear, though, is that in the past there have been many, many elephant types of all shapes and sizes. You can see some of them on the opposite page. The two species alive today, the African and Indian elephants, are a small reminder of a once numerous and widespread group.

Elephant evolution is sometimes traced back to a small pig-like creature called *Moeritherium* that lived 50 million years ago. But, although this shows us what the elephants' ancestors may have looked like, we cannot be sure it actually *was* their relation.

Palaeomastodon and *Phiomia*, which lived about 35 million years ago, are the first mammals we can confidently include in the elephant group, which is called the *Proboscidea*. These were large mammals with short trunks and tusks. After them, the main story of elephant evolution has been one of increasing body size – perhaps because this made them less vulnerable to enemies. The head and jaws also changed and became shorter, possibly because really big jaws were too heavy and awkward. As the jaws became shorter, the upper lip and nose became longer to form the trunk which could reach for and grip food.

To feed their large bodies, elephants also developed better teeth for grinding large quantities of plants and for coping with tough grasses. Today's elephants have huge molar teeth covered with many ridges. And to help them even further, they have three sets of these molars which appear one after the other during the animal's life. The third and last set of molars come into use when the elephant is about 30 years old, and as these teeth wear away the elephant's long life draws to a close...

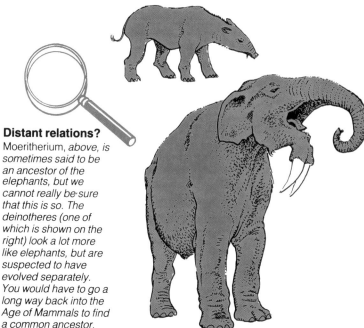

Distant relations?
Moeritherium, *above, is sometimes said to be an ancestor of the elephants, but we cannot really be·sure that this is so. The deinotheres (one of which is shown on the right) look a lot more like elephants, but are suspected to have evolved separately. You would have to go a long way back into the Age of Mammals to find a common ancestor.*

South America during the Pliocene

1 Thylacosmilus *was a fierce meat eating marsupial. It had long upper canine teeth (saber teeth), with deep flaps sticking out from the lower jaw to support and protect them.*

2 Toxodon *was one of the last of the primitive hoofed mammals to live in South America. The size of a rhino, with stumpy legs, it has been described by some scientists as a "gigantic guinea pig."*

3 Glyptodon *was an armadillo-like creature, up to 10 feet long, which was well protected by interlocking bony plates in its skin. Its large, strong molar teeth suggest that it ate grasses and other plants.*

4 Macrauchenia *belonged to the group of hoofed mammals called litopterns. This species was camel-like in appearance and possibly had the same habits.*

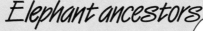

Elephant ancestors

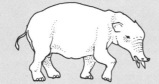

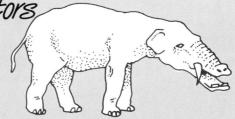

Palaeomastodon from 35 million years ago was about 6½ feet long. It had four long, shovel-like tusks in its jaw. The teeth were rather piglike, showing that it ate soft vegetation.

Phiomia also from about 35 million years ago, was 4 feet long. The shape of its fossil skull in the nose and upper jaw area suggests the beginnings of the elephant trunk.

Platybelodon was around 6½ feet tall, and lived from 20 million years ago. It had short upper tusks and blade-like lower tusks. Its jaws and mouth worked like a shovel to dig plants out of the ground.

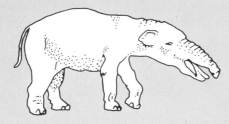

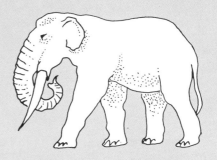

Gomphotherium lived about 15 to 20 million years ago. It was about 5 feet tall and had four tusks.

Ambelodon lived around 5 million years ago. It stood 6½ feet at the shoulder, and used its elongated "lips" to shovel food into its mouth.

Palaeoloxodon was big even for an elephant, standing 14 feet at the shoulder, with an overall height of perhaps 15 feet. It lived in forests and only died out about 250,000 years ago.

Dwarf elephants evolved on some islands, especially in the Mediterranean. They were similar to *Palaeoloxodon* but only 3 feet high.

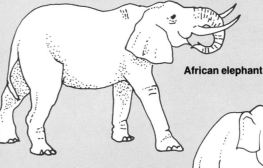

African elephant

Indian elephant

Mammoths were elephants that flourished on the Earth 2 million years ago. Some lived in warm climates, but when the Ice Ages came only the famous woolly mammoths could survive the cold. They developed the most ridged teeth of all elephants, presumably because of the tough, strong plants which grew in the cold conditions. Woolly mammoths were about 15 feet tall and, unlike all other elephants (as far as we know), they were covered in long hair for warmth. We know this because woolly mammoths have been found frozen solid in the ice of Siberia, perfectly preserved.

Today's African and **Indian** elephants are the only species that still exist. The African elephant is 12 feet tall at the shoulder, perhaps more, and has much larger ears than the Indian version.

The dawn of Darwin's Ideas

Darwin's voyage

Darwin traveled to South America and the Pacific on a ship called the Beagle. *The map on the right shows its passage around South America and the Galapagos Islands.*

On the shores of Patagonia, Darwin found many fossils, as you can see in the picture below. He dug up the fossilized bones of many extinct animals and study of these led him to form his theories about evolution.

Today nearly all palaeontologists accept the general idea of evolution. We almost take it for granted that animals and plants gradually change with time, as one generation follows another. Sometimes a particular kind of animal becomes extinct or changes into a completely new and different species.

One of the main reasons we believe in the idea of evolution is that we can imagine how it happens. As the world slowly changes, it suits some animals better than others. These well-adapted types thrive, while others die out. We call this "the survival of the fittest," and we owe the idea to the naturalist Charles Darwin.

In 1831 Darwin sailed around the world on a ship called the *Beagle*, which spent five years mapping the coasts of South America. The things that Darwin saw convinced him of the theory of evolution, even though people laughed at his ideas. He visited the Galapagos Islands, where he saw a variety of closely-related living species, and spent time in South America where he found many wonderful and unique mammal fossils. These were the most important parts of his voyage.

Darwin saw, first hand, just what odd and gigantic animals had lived in the area called Patagonia, and this made him think about how and why animals became extinct. He also studied the

Giant ground sloths

Darwin's finds included several gigantic ground sloths. Big as elephants, they are thought to have rested on their heavy back legs and pulled leaves and twigs to their mouths with their long-clawed hands and long tongues. *Megatherium* (right) was the biggest of all, at 19 feet long. Ground sloths survived in South America for over 30 million years, dying out only a few thousand years ago. Sometimes their "mummified" (dried out) remains are found in caves, along with their droppings, which show what they ate. The only sloths still living in South America today are the small, climbing tree sloths.

rocks and saw for himself clear evidence that the sea levels had changed, how rock layers had formed, and how fossils differed in various layers.

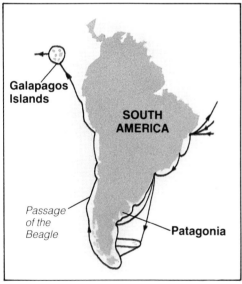

Galapagos Islands

SOUTH AMERICA

Passage of the Beagle

Patagonia

The reason for the uniqueness of the South American mammals is that for most of the Age of Mammals, South America was an island. Before the Age of Mammals all the continents had been joined together. But they split up and drifted apart and, early in mammal history, South America became separated from the rest.

The animals living in South America evolved along their own lines. The *marsupials*, under threat in other parts, did very well. But by 2 million years ago South America had drifted to its present position, joined to North America by the narrow Isthmus of Panama. In the struggles that followed, the South American animals generally came off worse. Big meat-eating marsupials such as *Thylacosmilus* (see page 30-31) were replaced by cats, dogs, and otters. Horses, guanacos, and deers took over from the primitive hoofed mammals. A few animals like the opossum and the armadillo traveled north and still live in North America. But generally the northerners took over and animals from the south became extinct.

Charles Darwin took many years to work on his evidence about the survival of the fittest. He saw nature as selecting those best fitted to the surroundings. Another naturalist, Alfred Wallace, also thought of this. In 1858 Darwin and Wallace wrote a scientific paper together. Then in 1859 Darwin published his book: *On the Origin of Species by Means of Natural Selection* (which is often called simply *The Origin of Species*). This became one of the most influential books ever published.

Charles Darwin
Darwin (1809-82) was only 22 years old when he joined the Beagle's *voyage as naturalist. His pioneering work has made the theory of evolution almost universally accepted.*

New mammals for old

Even though we may not know all the details, the general trends in evolution, between the mammals of 50 or 60 million years ago and those of today, are fairly clear.

For example, the early plant eaters such as *Coryphodon* and *Uintatherium* were heavily built, clumsy and had small brains. They were sitting suppers for the better carnivores of their day. Compare them to a modern horse or gazelle with its light build, speed, keen senses of sight, hearing, and smell, and its relatively large brain. It is easy to see how improvements like this helped in escaping from predators. But as the plant eaters changed, so did the meat eaters – they had to, or they would have died out.

There are, however, many evolutionary puzzles. Opossums have scarcely changed for 60 million years. Pangolins (scaly anteaters) and bats have remained almost the same for 50 million years or more. Why? Is it that evolution quickly came up with a "first-time hit," a creature so perfectly in tune with its way of life that no more improvements were possible? Or is it just their good fortune that no other animals have evolved to knock them from their positions?

At the other end of the scale we know of mammal groups that have never stopped changing. Their fossils show that one type evolved into another, and so on up to the present day. The even-toed hoofed mammals make up a group that has evolved like this. They existed in many different forms 30 million years ago, developing into the huge variety of antelopes and others that wander the African plains today. What's the secret of their success?

Well, we must admit that there are no good answers to these questions at the moment, but there are plenty of theories. Perhaps a new Charles Darwin will come along to pick up the clues and discover more of the secrets of the past.

Even-toed hoofed mammals

There are so many species of even-toed fossil mammals that it is difficult to keep track of them all. The oreodonts such as *Merycoidodon* (left) and cainotheres like *Dichobune* (above) were early members of the group. Today, the same group contains dozens of species – of pigs, hippos, camels, sheep, deer, oxen, and many, many antelopes.

INDEX